CSS

Basic Fundamental Guide for Beginners

TABLE OF CONTENTS

Introduction

Congratulations on purchasing *CSS: Basic Fundamental Guide For Beginners* and thank you for doing so! Whether you're interested in learning CSS to enhance a personal website or you'd just like to gain a better understanding of how your browser does what it does. This book is a great starting point. With its many examples and simple to understand explanations, you'll soon be on your way to creating unique web pages that function smoothly and efficiently!

Before diving into this book, a basic idea of HTML is a plus and how to use it to create a simple web page. Combine that knowledge with an editor and a browser and you're ready to get started! Over the course of this book, you'll not only learn the art of using CSS selectors in making our HTML web pages more interactive, you'll also discover techniques for creating beautiful page layouts. When it comes to interacting with users, having an approachable and easy-to-use website is crucial. By the end of this book, you can be confident that your web pages are just as simple to navigate as they are appealing to view.

There are many books available on this subject, so thanks again for choosing this one. Good luck, and have fun taking off with CSS!

Chapter 1

Taking Off With CSS

If you have ever written HTML to create a web page previously, it is highly likely that you've also used CSS. CSS stands literally for Cascading Style Sheets, and it is used in web pages alongside HTML to define page styles and layouts. Need to change the default font of a paragraph? Wish that picture had a border? Would a cool animation really bring your page to life? You can do all of that using CSS!

With the examples here, just get one text editor (like Notepad or TextEdit) to write some HTML and CSS and a browser (like Google Chrome, Internet Explorer, or Mozilla Firefox) to view what you've written.

How do CSS and HTML work together?

Generally speaking, your web browser will use the rules that you set within your CSS to determine how to display a web page. An HTML file will provide the content and define the content's type, and a CSS file will assign different styles to those different content types. CSS uses what are called properties and selectors to assign these styles. A property can be something like an element's size or color. A selector is what CSS uses to refer to an element or group of elements in order to assign them a style.

You can contain all of the rules for how to display the elements in your HTML document within a separate file called a stylesheet. A stylesheet will have a .css file extension, and you will link to it within the <head> element of your HTML file. For instance, consider the following HTML:

```
<!DOCTYPE html>
<html>
   <head>
           <title>A CSS Example!</title>
   </head>
   <body>
           <h1>A big important heading</h1>
           <p>An ordinary paragraph</p>
   </body>
</html>
```

If you save the above HTML in a file with a .html extension and then open it using a browser, it won't look very impressive -- just black text on a white background. However, you can change that with a little bit of CSS. Take a look at the following:

```
h1 {
    background-color: red;
    color: white;
    border: 2px dashed blue;
}
p {
    background-color: grey;
    color: aqua;
}
```

Save this CSS in a file called styles.css. Now, we'll just have to add one line into the previous HTML example, thereby connecting CSS stylesheet with the HTML file. In the <head> element, insert a <link> element as follows:

```html
<!DOCTYPE html>
<html>
   <head>
          <title>A CSS Example!</title>
          <link rel="stylesheet" href="styles.css">
   </head>
   <body>
          <h1>A big important heading</h1>
          <p>An ordinary paragraph</p>
   </body>
</html>
```

Save this HTML with a .html extension in the same folder where you just saved styles.css. Now when you open your HTML using your browser, it will look a little more interesting:

A big important heading

An ordinary paragraph

So what did we just do? In our .css file, we defined two rules. Both rules start with a selector and then contain declarations, which define the values for certain properties. The selector for the first rule is **h1**, and the rule contains three declarations: the first declaration generates red background color, white color emanates from the next, and the third declaration creates a dashed blue border around the element. The selector for the second rule is **p**, and it contains two declarations: the first declaration sets the background color to grey, and the second declaration sets the text color to aqua. These rules will apply to every element in your HTML file that use <h1> or <p> tags.

How can I use CSS with my HTML?

In the last section, you put some CSS into a separate file from your HTML document and then linked to that file in order to use the styles it defined. When you use CSS in this manner, it's called an external stylesheet. In most cases, this is the method that you should use when styling your websites. Not only does this method allow you to efficiently organize all the styling rules for your web page in one place, it also allows you to use the same rules for multiple pages by linking to the same .css file from multiple .html files. That means that even if your website contains 100 pages, you can control the style for all of them just by altering a single .css file!

If for some reason you don't want to use an external stylesheet, you have a couple of other options for using CSS to style your HTML documents. Before we look at those options, first take a moment to remember how the HTML and CSS looked using the external stylesheet method.

Some HTML:

```
<!DOCTYPE html>
<html>
    <head>
            <title>A CSS Example!</title>
            <link rel="stylesheet" href="styles.css">
    </head>
    <body>
            <h1>A big important heading</h1>
            <p>An ordinary paragraph</p>
            <h2>A less important heading to introduce a list</h2>
            <ul>
                    A list of assorted objects:
                    <li>a hairbrush</li>
                    <li>a skeleton key</li>
                    <li>a cat</li>
                    <li>a gaming console</li>
                    <li>a pancake</li>
            <ul>
    </body>
</html>
```

Some CSS:

```
h1 {
    background-color: red;
    color: white;
    border: 2px dashed blue;
}
h2 {
    background-color: purple;
    color: yellow;
}
p {
    background-color: grey;
    color: aqua;
}
ul {
    text-decoration: underline;
    border: 1px solid green;
}
li {
    text-decoration: bold;
}
```

The first alternative to using an external stylesheet that we'll take a look at is called an internal stylesheet. Instead of placing a <link> element within the <head> element of your HTML document, you'll instead use a <style> element to contain the CSS declarations. To create the same page as the example above using an internal stylesheet, your HTML document would look something like this:

```
<!DOCTYPE html>
<html>
    <head>
            <title>A CSS Example!</title>
            <style>
                    h1 {
```

```
    background-color: red;
    color: white;
    border: 2px dashed blue;
}
h2 {
    background-color: purple;
    color: yellow;
}
p {
    background-color: grey;
    color: aqua;
}
ul {
    text-decoration: underline;
    border: 1px solid green;
}
li {
    text-decoration: bold;
}
        </style>
    </head>
    <body>
        <h1>A big important heading</h1>
        <p>An ordinary paragraph</p>
        <h2>A less important heading to introduce a list</h2>
        <ul>
            A list of assorted objects:
            <li>a hairbrush</li>
            <li>a skeleton key</li>
            <li>a cat</li>
            <li>a gaming console</li>
            <li>a pancake</li>
        <ul>
    </body>
</html>
```

This method has the benefit of containing all of the styling information you need in the same document as your HTML. Changing the styles within the <style> element will apply them to the <h1> and <p> elements throughout your .html document. However, if you want to create multiple pages with the same style rules, you'll have to put the CSS into each file individually. Then, if you decide you want to change something, you'll have to change it in multiple files.

A third option for applying CSS to you HTML document is via inline styles. Inline styles only affect a single HTML element, and they are defined within the **style** attribute in the start tag of an element. To create the same page as above using inline styles, you would have to do the following:

```
<!DOCTYPE html>
<html>
    <head>
            <title>A CSS Example!</title>
    </head>
    <body>
            <h1 style="background-color: red; color: white; border: 2px dashed blue;">A big important heading</h1>
            <p style="background-color: grey; color: aqua;">An ordinary paragraph</p>
    </body>
            <h2 style="background-color: purple; color: yellow">A less important heading to introduce a list</h2>
            <ul style="text-decoration: underline; border: 1px solid green;" >
                    A list of assorted objects:
                    <li style="text-decoration: bold;">a hairbrush</li>
                    <li style="text-decoration: bold;">a skeleton key</li>
                    <li style="text-decoration: bold;">a cat</li>
```

```
            <li   style="text-decoration:   bold;">a   gaming
console</li>
            <li          style="text-decoration:          bold;">a
pancake</li>
      <ul>
</html>
```

Although this might be a reasonable option in certain restrictive circumstances, it is generally not a good idea to use inline styles. If you decide to change any of the styles on your website, you won't just have to update each affected page -- you'll have to update each affected *element*. Additionally, having the styles defined within the start tag of each element tends to clutter up your HTML file and make it harder to read and understand.

How should I format my CSS?

You've already seen a couple of simple examples of how to properly format your CSS in the previous sections. Take a look at the following components to gain a better understanding of CSS syntax:

Property: A property is an identifier that is used to indicate what feature of an element you want to style. Properties are descriptive and meant to be easy for a human to read and understand. Some examples of properties include size, font, color, and border. There are over 300 properties available to use in CSS! CSS properties are case sensitive and they all use US spelling -- color doesn't work, but color does.

Value: A value is assigned to a property to define what its specific style should be. A color property could have a value of blue or red, for instance. The available values depend on which property they're defining. Like properties, values are case sensitive.

Declaration: A CSS declaration is the pairing of a property with a value. A declaration is formatted as follows, with the property first, a colon, and then the value:

color: blue;

background-color: purple;

width: 100%;

font-family: courier;

It's worth noting here that not every value is valid for every property. Each property has its own list of acceptable values. If you try to use an invalid property or value in your declaration, the browser will simply ignore the whole declaration.

Declaration block: A declaration block contains zero or more CSS declarations. The declaration blocks are contained in {} brackets and separated by semicolons. The final declaration in a declaration block doesn't need to end with a semicolon, but that is better to ensure consistency:

```
{color: blue;
    background-color: aqua;
    border-left: 1px dashed green;
    width: 100%;
    text-decoration: underline;
}
```

Ruleset: A ruleset or rule is the pairing of a declaration block with a CSS selector or group of selectors. This pairing is accomplished simply by placing the selector or group of selectors before the opening {bracket of the declaration block. Each selector in a group of selectors should be separated by a comma:

```
h1 {
    background-color: black;
    color: white;
    font-family: courier;
}
```

```
h2, p {
    background-color: grey;
    color: aqua;
    font-family: verdana;
}
```

If any of the selectors in a group of selectors is invalid, the browser will skip over it. However, the browser will still apply the styles set in the declaration block to the remaining selectors in the group.

In addition to understanding and properly formatting your CSS rules, it is also generally a good idea to use whitespace to your advantage within your .css files. Although it isn't necessary to create a functioning web page, using line breaks, tabs, and spaces in your file can make it readable and simple to alter if the need arises. For instance, this CSS:

```
h1 {
background-color:red;
color:white;
font-family: courier;
border:2px dashed blue;
}
p {
background-color:grey;
font-family: verdana;
color:aqua;
}
```
and this CSS:
```
h1{background-color:red;color:white;font-
family:courier;border:2px     dashed     blue;}p{background-
color:grey;font-family:verdana;color:aqua;}
```

will both define the same styles for your web pages. However, it is much easier to see and understand what is being done in the first example, and it would be much easier to make any changes if needed.

Chapter 2

Using CSS Selectors

In the last chapter, you had a chance to work with some basic CSS examples, and you learned that one or more selectors should come before a declaration block. Now, let's take a look at some of the different selector types and how they can be used to apply styles to your web pages:

Simple Selectors

A simple selector is used to refer to a single or multiple elements based on their ID, their class, or their type. A simple selector could look like any one of the following:

p

h4

ol

.someclass

.important

p.error

#q1

#input4

*

The first kind of simple selector is very common and is called a type selector or an element selector. Type selectors are not case sensitive, and they are a simple way to refer to all of the elements of the same type within an HTML document, like all the type 1 headings or all the ordered lists. For the following HTML:

```
<!DOCTYPE html>
<html>
   <head>
          <title>CSS Type Selectors</title>
          <link rel="stylesheet" href="styles.css">
   </head>
   <body>
          <p>A paragraph with a defined color and background
color</p>
          <ol>
                 A list with a border:
                 <li>square</li>
                 <li>circle</li>
                 <li>triangle</li>
          </ol>
   </body>
</html>
```

the following CSS uses the type selectors **p** and **ol** to style the <p> and <ol> elements:

```
p {
   background-color: blue;
   color: yellow;
   font-family: courier;
   text-decoration: bold;
}
ol {
   border: 1px solid green;
}
```

Another simple selector is the class selector. Instead of using the element type, the class selector uses a class name to refer to an element. In the .css file, the class selector is a period followed by the class name. In the .html file, the class name is written in the **class** attribute within an element's start tag. For example, for the following HTML:

```
<!DOCTYPE html>
<html>
    <head>
            <title>CSS Class Selectors</title>
            <link rel="stylesheet" href="styles.css">
    </head>
    <body>
            <ul>
                    A list with items of different classes:
                    <li class="shape first important">square</li>
                    <li class="shape second important">circle</li>
                    <li class="shape third">triangle</li>
            </ul>
    </body>
</html>
```

the following CSS uses the .shape, .first, .second, .third, and .important class selectors to style the items in the list. An element can have multiple classes, and it will use the styles assigned to all of its classes:

```
.shape {
    background-color: red;
    color: aqua;
}
.first {
    text-decoration: underline;
}
.second {
}
```

14

```
.third {
    font-family: courier;
}
.important {
    font-weight: bold;
}
```

The resulting list will look like so:

A list with items of different classes:

You can also use class selectors such as **p.error** or **p.valid** to refer to classes within a certain type of element. In this way, you could set a style for the error class that displays differently when it is a <p> element as opposed to a <div> or another type of element.

The third kind of simple selector is the ID selector. Similar to a class selector, an id selector refers to an id that is defined within the start tag of an element. However, while multiple elements can have the same class, only one element can have anID. If you attempt to assign the same id to multiple elements, you might encounter errors, or the browser might only accept the first instance. Take a look at the following HTML:

```
<!DOCTYPE html>
<html>
  <head>
        <title>CSS Class Selectors</title>
        <link rel="stylesheet" href="styles.css">
  </head>
  <body>
        <p id="george">George likes the color blue.</p>
        <p id="amy">Amy likes green.</p>
```

```
    </body>
</html>
```

and the following CSS:

```
#george {
color: blue;
}
#amy {
color: green;
}
```

In the above example, you can see thatID selectors are written using the # symbol followed by the id value. Any element can be assigned a unique id within its start tag.

The final kind of simple selector that we will cover in this book is called the universal selector, which is simply written as the * symbol. The universal selector applies the styles defined in its declaration block to every element on the page. It is very uncommon to have a situation in which you should use the universal selector, and it can cause large web pages to have significantly poorer performance. A simple example could use the following HTML:

```
<!DOCTYPE html>
<html>
    <head>
            <title>CSS Class Selectors</title>
            <link rel="stylesheet" href="styles.css">
    </head>
    <body>
            <h1>A large and important heading</h1>
            <p>A  regular  paragraph  with  some  <b>bold</b>,
<i>italicized</i>, and <u>underlined</u> elements.</p>
    </body>
</html>
```

and the following CSS:

```
* {
    border: 1px double black;
    color: purple;
}
```

to create a page that looks like this:

Attribute Selectors

A somewhat more complex kind of selector is called an attribute selector, and it works by matching the value of an element's attribute. The attributes are contained within the start tag of an element in the .html file and are written in [] brackets in the .css stylesheet. For instance, take a look at the following HTML:

```
<!DOCTYPE html>
<html>
    <head>
        <title>CSS Class Selectors</title>
        <link rel="stylesheet" href="styles.css">
    </head>
    <body>
        A list of assorted things:
        <ul>
            <li thing-category="shape" thing-color="blue">square</li>
            <li thing-category="number" thing-color="none">four</li>
```

```
                    <li        thing-category="number"        thing-
color="none">17</li>
                    <li        thing-category="shape"         thing-
color="green">circle</li>
                    <li        thing-category="animal"        thing-
color="white">bunny</li>
            </ul>
      </body>
</html>
```

and the following CSS:

```
[thing-category] {
    background-color: aqua;
}
[thing-category=shape] {
    text-decoration: bold;
}
[thing-color] {
    color: red;
}
[thing-color=blue] {
    color: blue;
}
[thing-color=green] {
    color: green;
}
```

When viewed with a browser, your page should look similar to this:

A list of assorted things:

- square
- four
- 17
- circle
- bunny

In the above example, you can see how you can use attribute selectors in a couple of different ways. If you only list the attribute as the selector, the corresponding declaration block applies the contained styles. It does this to all, irrespective of the attribute value. On the other hand, if you list both an attribute and a value as the selector, the styles in the declaration block are only applied to elements that have that attribute set to that value.

Multiple Selectors

If you would like to use the same styles for more than one set of elements, you can pair multiple selectors with the same declaration block by separating them with commas. For example, if you use the following HTML:

```
<!DOCTYPE html>
<html>
    <head>
            <title>CSS Class Selectors</title>
            <link rel="stylesheet" href="styles.css">
    </head>
    <body>
            <h1>A big and important heading</h1>
            <h2>A less important heading</h2>
            <h3>An even less important heading</h3>
            <h4>A somewhat unimportant heading</h4>
            <h5>An even more unimportant heading</h5>
            <h6>A small and very unimportant heading</h6>
    </body>
</html>
```

with the following CSS:

```
h1, h3, h5 {
    background-color: grey;
}
h2, h4, h6 {
    color: blue;
}
```

your output will look something like this:

A big and important heading

A less important heading

An even less important heading

A somewhat unimportant heading

An even more unimportant heading

A small and very unimportant heading

Great! You now have an idea of how to use some common and useful selectors to apply custom styles to elements and groups of elements. Play around with the techniques you just learned. Can you figure out how to assign the same style to a class and an id without rewriting the declaration block? How does an element display if you assign different values to the same property within different declaration blocks? What happens if an element is nested within another element? Set up these scenarios in your text editor and find out!

Chapter 3

CSS Layout Basics

In the last chapters, you've had the opportunity to use CSS rules to define the styles for elements in your HTML documents. CSS doesn't just define appearance attributes like colors and borders, however. It is also a valuable tool in deciding how elements are laid out on a web page. CSS uses a box model to determine where to place each element -- every element is considered as a rectangular box shape, and those boxes are placed in relation to one another. Each element "box" contains the element content, some space called padding between the content and a border, the border itself, and then surrounding space called a margin. Take a look at some of the following defining properties:

Width and Height: The height and width properties set the height and width of the area where the content of an element box is displayed. This content can be something like the text or image content of an element, or it could include other boxes nested inside. Widths are measured using either pixels (written as 100px, for instance) or by the percentage of the page they cover (a box with a width of 50% would span half the total page width). Heights are measured using pixels and don't use percentages.

You can also set maximum or minimum values for your content boxes instead of defining a size using pixels or percentages. These maximum and minimum values can be set using properties like max-width, max-height, min-width, and min-height. Play around with these attributes to determine which are best for managing the content of your specific

web page. Check out the following examples for defining the size of a
<div> element:

```
div {
    height: 225px;
    width: 50%;
}
div {
    max-height: 500px;
    min-height: 20px;
    max-width: 300px;
    min-width: 15px;
}
```

Do not set the width or height of your content box to a value that is greater than the size of the browser window in which you are viewing your page. If you do so, the content box will overflow outside of the window and you will need to use the up/down and left/right scroll bars to view the entire box.

Padding: The padding of a content box is the space between the content itself and the edge of the box where a border would be. You can define the padding on each side of your content box individually by using the padding-left, padding-right, padding-top, and padding-bottom properties. Alternatively, you can set the padding for all four sides at once by using the padding property followed by the top, right, bottom, and left padding values. Take a look at each of these methods below for styling a <div> element:

```
div {
    padding-left: 125px;
    padding-right: 20px;
    padding-top: 55px;
    padding-bottom: 110px;
}
div {
    padding: 55px 20px 110px 125px;
}
```

Both of the above rulesets accomplish the same thing. You can also have a padding property that contains 3, 2, or even 1 value instead of 4. If a padding property contains 3 values, the first value corresponds to the padding-top value, the second value corresponds to the padding-right and padding-left values, and the third value corresponds to the padding-bottom value. If a padding property contains 2 values, the first value corresponds to the padding-top and padding-bottom values and the second value corresponds to the padding-left and padding-right values. If a padding property only contains a single value, that value is used for all four sides.

Border: The border for a content box is located between the padding and the margin of the box. The default border size for an element is 0, which would display as nothing, or invisible. However, you can use border-width, border-color, and border-style properties to define a border with a specific thickness, style, and color. You can also use the border, border-left, border-right, border-top, or border-bottom properties to define the style, color, and thickness of a border on one or all sides of your content box. If you'd like to instead set a specific border property on only one side of your content box, you can do that as well by using properties such as border-top-width, border-top-color, or border-top-style. Take a look at some of the ways you might define the styles for the border of a <div> element:

```
div {
    border-left: 2px solid black;
    border-right: 5px solid black;
    border-top: 1px solid red;
    border-bottom: 3px solid red;
}
div {
    border: 2px dashed green;
}
```

```
div {
    border-top-style: dotted;
    border-top-color: green;
    border-top-width: 4px;
    border-bottom-style: double;
    border-bottom-color: purple;
    border-bottom-width: 1px;
    border-left-style: dashed;
    border-left-color: yellow;
    border-left-width: 3px;
    border-right-style: ridge;
    border-right-color: aqua;
    border-right-width: 2px;
}
div {
    border-weight: 2px;
    border-color: blue;
}
```

It is worth noting here that, by default, the background color of an element will extend to the outer edge of the border.

Margin: An element box's margin envelopes the outside margin and demarcates the box from other entities, sort of like an outer padding. You can set the top, right, left, and bottom margins for an element all at once using the margin property, or you can set them individually using the margin-top, margin-bottom, margin-left, and margin-right properties.

The margins from separate elements within a web page can push up against one another and use margin collapsing when they touch. With margin collapsing, the distance between two touching element boxes becomes the larger of the two touching margins instead of the sum of the two touching margins.

Some examples for defining the margins of a <div> element are as follows:

```
div {
    margin: 20px 30px 15px 10px;
}
div {
    margin-top: 20px;
    margin-right: 30px;
    margin-bottom: 15px;
    margin-left: 10px;
}
```

Similarly to the padding property, the margin property can have anywhere from one to four values. If the margin property has four values, they correspond to the margin's top, right, bottom, and left values, in that order. If the margin property has three values, the first value corresponds to the top margin, the second value corresponds to the left and right margins, and the third value corresponds to the bottom margin. If the margin property has two values, the first value corresponds to the top and bottom margins, and the second value corresponds to the left and right margins. If the margin property only has one value, that value corresponds to all the four margins of the element box.

Using the box model, it is easy to determine to a total actual size that an element will take up on a page. To determine the element's height, add the content box height, the top padding, the bottom padding, the top border, the bottom border, the top margin, and the bottom margin. Similarly, to determine the element's width, add the content box width, the left padding, the right padding, the left border, the right border, the left margin, and the right margin. Note that this method will give you the total space that an element will take up on the web page. If you would instead like to know how big the element will look, perform the same calculations as above without adding in the top margin, the bottom margin, the left margin, or the right margin.

Position: With the position attribute, you can define the location of an element on your page. There are several different values for the position attribute, including static, fixed, relative, absolute, and sticky. These positions are then defined using the top, bottom, right, and left attributes to set the top margin edge, bottom margin edge, right margin edge, or left margin edge location within your page.

The static value is the default for the position attribute, and doesn't really do anything special to the positioning of the element; it will just flow normally with the page:

```
div {
    position: static;
}
```

The fixed value puts an element in a fixed position relative to the viewing port for your web page, and uses the top, bottom, left, and right attributes to define the said position. The following example would place the <div> element into the bottom right corner of your browser window:

```
div {
    position: fixed;
    width: 75px;
    height: 50px;
    right: 0;
    bottom: 0;
}
```

The relative value sets an element's position relative to where it would normally be located on the page and leaves a space in the page where the element would normally be. The following example would move the <div> element over 75 pixels from its default position:

```
div {
    position: relative;
    left: 75px;
}
```

The absolute value allows an element to be positioned in a specific location based on an ancestor's location or the body of the document if no ancestor is present. The following example could be used to position the "little" div in the bottom right corner of the "big" div:

```
div.big {
    position: relative;
    width: 450px;
    height: 250px;
}
div.little {
    position: absolute;
    bottom: 0;
    right: 0;
    width: 150px;
    height: 75px;
}

<!DOCTYPE html>
<html>
    <body>
            <div class="big">
This div is big and has a relative position
<div class="little">
This div is smaller and its position is relative to the big div it is contained in</div>
</div>
</div>
    </body>
</html>
```

The sticky value allows an element to have a position based on a user's scroll position. A sticky element will have a relative position until a user scrolls past it, and then it will "stick" to one position in the viewing window. The following example will cause the <div> element to stay 50 pixels down from the top of the screen once a user scrolls to it:

```
div {
    position: sticky;
    top: 50px;
}
```

Float: The float property in CSS can be a useful tool when defining your page layouts. One of the most common uses of the float property is to wrap text around images or display images side by side. Or, if you'd like, you can even use the float property to set the layout of your entire web page! The following CSS would cause the <img> elements to float to the right of the text within a paragraph, and allow the text to wrap around the image naturally once it gets long enough:

```
img {
    float: right;
}

<!DOCTYPE html>
<html>
    <body>
            <p><img src="shapes.png">A bunch of text!</p>
    </body>
</html>
```

Clear: The clear property is used along with the float property to further control the layout of a web page. By using the clear property, you can disallow floating elements to the left and right of an element. For instance, the following CSS would make it so that no elements are allowed to float on either side of the <div> element:

```
div {
    clear: both;
}
```

By default, the clear property has a value of none; that is, floating elements are allowed both to the left and to the right of the element.

Let's take a look at some examples of web pages using the properties discussed in this chapter. For the first page, copy and paste or manually type the following HTML into your text editor and save it with a .html extension:

```
<!DOCTYPE html>
<html>
    <head>
        <title>CSS Layout Example</title>
        <link rel="stylesheet" href="styles.css">
    </head>
    <body>
        <div class="news">
            This could tell users about a cool new update for your site!
        </div>
        <div class="pageheader">
            <h1>The header for your webpage!</h1>
        </div>
        <div class="column menu">
            <ul>
                <li>An item in your page menu</li>
                <li>A second item in your page menu</li>
                <li>A third item in your page menu</li>
                <li>A fourth item in your page menu</li>
                <li>A fifth item in your page menu</li>
            </ul>
        </div>
        <div class="column content">
            <h1>This could be a heading for some content on your page</h1>
```

```
            <p>This paragraph could welcome users to your
website.</p>
            <p>This could be an interesting paragraph about
a hobby or an interest that your page is about.</p>
            <p>This could be a followup paragraph for the
first.</p>
            <p>This paragraph could give users some
instructions on how to navigate your website.</p>
        </div>
        <div class="pagefooter">
            <p>Here is some text in the footer of your
webpage!</p>
        </div>
    </body>
</html>
```

Then, copy and paste or manually type the following CSS into a separate file in your text editor and save it at styles.css:

```
.pageheader, .pagefooter {
    clear: both;
    background-color: black;
    color: white;
    padding: 20px;
}
.column {
    float: left;
}
.menu {
    width: 20%;
    padding: 10px;
}
.content {
    width: 75%;
}
```

```
.menu ul {
    list-style-type: none;
    margin: 0;
    padding: 0;
}
.menu li {
    padding: 10px;
    margin-bottom: 10px;
    background-color: blue;
    color: aqua;
    text-decoration: bold;
    text-align: center;
}
.news {
    position: sticky;
    background-color: yellow;
    text-align: center;
    top: 20px;
    margin: 0px 5%;
    height: 20px;
    width: 90%;
    border: 2px dashed green;
}
```

Make sure that you saved the HTML file and the CSS file in the same folder, or put the CSS into the <head> element of your HTML document, as in this case:

```
<!DOCTYPE html>
<html>
    <head>
            <title>CSS Layout Example</title>
            <style>
.pageheader, .pagefooter {
    clear: both;
    background-color: black;
```

```css
    color: white;
    padding: 20px;
}
.column {
    float: left;
}
.menu {
    width: 20%;
    padding: 10px;
}
.content {
    width: 75%;
}
.menu ul {
    list-style-type: none;
    margin: 0;
    padding: 0;
}
.menu li {
    padding: 10px;
    margin-bottom: 10px;
    background-color: blue;
    color: aqua;
    text-decoration: bold;
    text-align: center;
}
.news {
    position: sticky;
    background-color: yellow;
    text-align: center;
    top: 20px;
    margin: 0px 5%;
    height: 20px;
    width: 90%;
    border: 2px dashed green;
```

```
}
        </style>
    </head>
    <body>

        <div class="news">
            This could tell users about a cool new update for
your site!
        </div>

        <div class="pageheader">
            <h1>The header for your webpage!</h1>
        </div>

        <div class="column menu">
            <ul>
                <li>An item in your page menu</li>
                <li>A    second    item    in    your    page
menu</li>
                <li>A third item in your page menu</li>
                <li>A    fourth    item    in    your    page
menu</li>
                <li>A fifth item in your page menu</li>
            </ul>
        </div>

        <div class="column content">
            <h1>This could be a heading for some content
on your page</h1>
            <p>This paragraph could welcome users to your
website.</p>
            <p>This could be an interesting paragraph about
a hobby or an interest that your page is about.</p>
            <p>This could be a followup paragraph for the
first.</p>
```

```
        <p>This paragraph could give users some
instructions on how to navigate your website.</p>
        </div>

        <div class="pagefooter">
            <p>Here is some text in the footer of your
webpage!</p>
        </div>
    </body>
</html>
```

Then, open the HTML file with your browser. The resulting page should look similar to this:

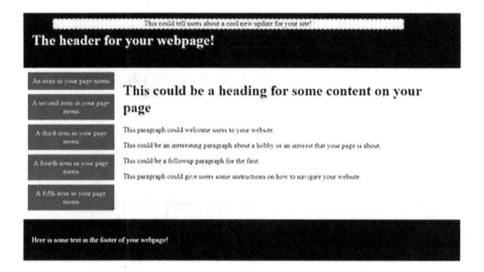

For this next example, copy and paste or manually type the following HTML into your text editor and save it with an .html extension:

```
<!DOCTYPE html>
<html>
    <head>
        <title>CSS Layout Example</title>
        <link rel="stylesheet" href="styles.css">
    </head>
```

```
<body>

    <div class="pagealert">
    This box will always show at the bottom of the
page. Use it for news or alerts!
    </div>

    <div class="pageheader">
    <h1>Put some text here to display in your page
header!</h1>
    </div>

    <ul>
    <li><a class="active" href="#home">A menu
item</a></li>
    <li><a    href="#page1">A    second    menu
item</a></li>
    <li><a    href="#page2">A    third    menu
item</a></li>
    <li><a    href="#page3">A    fourth    menu
item</a></li>
    </ul>

    <div class="content">
    <h1>This could be a heading for some content
on your page</h1>
    <p>This paragraph could welcome users to your
website.</p>
    <p>This could be an interesting paragraph about
a hobby or an interest that your page is about.</p>
    <p>This could be a followup paragraph for the
first.</p>
    <p>This  paragraph  could  give  users  some
instructions on how to navigate your website.</p>
    </div>
```

```
<img class="galleryitem" src="shapes.png">
<img class="galleryitem" src="rectangle.png">
<img class="galleryitem" src="triangle.png">
<img class="galleryitem" src="oval.png">
<img class="galleryitem" src="shapes.png">
<img class="galleryitem" src="rectangle.png">
<img class="galleryitem" src="triangle.png">
<img class="galleryitem" src="oval.png">
<img class="galleryitem" src="shapes.png">
<img class="galleryitem" src="rectangle.png">
<img class="galleryitem" src="triangle.png">
<img class="galleryitem" src="oval.png">
<img class="galleryitem" src="shapes.png">
<img class="galleryitem" src="rectangle.png">
<img class="galleryitem" src="triangle.png">
<img class="galleryitem" src="oval.png">

<div class="content">
        <p>This paragraph could contain descriptions
about the photos in your gallery.</p>
        </div>

        <div class="pagefooter">
                <p>Here is some text in the footer of your
webpage!</p>
        </div>
    </body>
</html>
```

Then, copy and paste or manually type the following CSS into a separate file in your text editor and save it at styles.css:

```css
.pageheader, .pagefooter {
    clear: both;
    background-color: grey;
    color: aqua;
    font-family: arial;
    padding: 15px;
}
.pageheader {
    font-size: 28px;
}
.pagefooter {
    margin-bottom: 50px;
    text-align: center;
}
.galleryitem {
    float: left;
    width: 31%;
    margin: 1%;
    border: 1px solid green;
}
.content {
    float: left;
    width: 100%;
}
ul {
    list-style-type: none;
    margin: 0;
    padding: 0;
    overflow: hidden;
    background-color: #333;
}
li {
    float: left;
}
li a {
```

```css
    display: inline-block;
    color: white;
    text-align: center;
    padding: 14px 16px;
    text-decoration: none;
}
li a:hover {
    background-color: orange;
}
.active {
    background-color: black;
}
.pagealert {
    position: fixed;
    background-color: red;
    text-align: center;
    text-decoration: bold;
    color: white;
    bottom: 20px;
    margin: 0px 25%;
    width: 50%;
    border: 3px double black;
}
```

Make sure that you saved the HTML file and the CSS file in the same folder, or just include the CSS in the HTML <head> element, like so:

```html
<!DOCTYPE html>
<html>
    <head>
            <title>CSS Layout Example</title>
            <style>
.pageheader, .pagefooter {
    clear: both;
    background-color: grey;
    color: aqua;
```

```css
    font-family: arial;
    padding: 15px;
}
.pageheader {
    font-size: 28px;
}
.pagefooter {
    margin-bottom: 50px;
    text-align: center;
}
.galleryitem {
    float: left;
    width: 31%;
    margin: 1%;
    border: 1px solid green;
}
.content {
    float: left;
    width: 100%;
}
ul {
    list-style-type: none;
    margin: 0;
    padding: 0;
    overflow: hidden;
    background-color: #333;
}
li {
    float: left;
}
li a {
    display: inline-block;
    color: white;
    text-align: center;
    padding: 14px 16px;
```

```css
    text-decoration: none;
}
li a:hover {
    background-color: orange;
}
.active {
    background-color: black;
}
.pagealert {
    position: fixed;
    background-color: red;
    text-align: center;
    text-decoration: bold;
    color: white;
    bottom: 20px;
    margin: 0px 25%;
    width: 50%;
    border: 3px double black;
}
        </style>
    </head>
    <body>

        <div class="pagealert">
            This box will always show at the bottom of the
page. Use it for news or alerts!
        </div>

        <div class="pageheader">
            <h1>Put some text here to display in your page
header!</h1>
        </div>

        <ul>
```

```html
            <li><a class="active" href="#home">A menu item</a></li>
            <li><a href="#page1">A second menu item</a></li>
            <li><a href="#page2">A third menu item</a></li>
            <li><a href="#page3">A fourth menu item</a></li>
        </ul>

        <div class="content">
            <h1>This could be a heading for some content on your page</h1>
            <p>This paragraph could welcome users to your website.</p>
            <p>This could be an interesting paragraph about a hobby or an interest that your page is about.</p>
            <p>This could be a followup paragraph for the first.</p>
            <p>This paragraph could give users some instructions on how to navigate your website.</p>
        </div>

        <img class="galleryitem" src="shapes.png">
        <img class="galleryitem" src="rectangle.png">
        <img class="galleryitem" src="triangle.png">
        <img class="galleryitem" src="oval.png">
        <img class="galleryitem" src="shapes.png">
        <img class="galleryitem" src="rectangle.png">
        <img class="galleryitem" src="triangle.png">
        <img class="galleryitem" src="oval.png">
        <img class="galleryitem" src="shapes.png">
        <img class="galleryitem" src="rectangle.png">
        <img class="galleryitem" src="triangle.png">
        <img class="galleryitem" src="oval.png">
```

```
<img class="galleryitem" src="shapes.png">
<img class="galleryitem" src="rectangle.png">
<img class="galleryitem" src="triangle.png">
<img class="galleryitem" src="oval.png">

<div class="content">
    <p>This paragraph could contain descriptions
about the photos in your gallery.</p>
    </div>

<div class="pagefooter">
    <p>Here is some text in the footer of your
webpage!</p>
    </div>
  </body>
</html>
```

Now, open the HTML file with your browser. The resulting page should look similar to this:

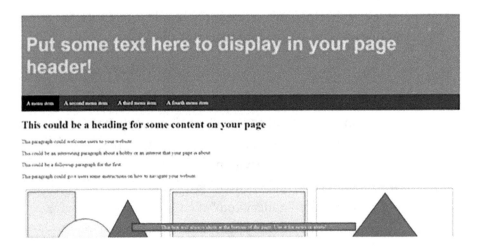

Once you have this page opened in your browser, see what happens if you scroll down the page or resize the browser window. For some practice, see if you can create a .css file that contains elements that retain their size when the window is made smaller or larger.

Chapter 4

Polishing Your Web Pages With CSS

In order to ensure that your web pages are displaying properly, it's important to frequently check your HTML and CSS files and debug them when necessary. Both HTML and CSS are permissive, so you don't have to worry about "breaking" you web page if you make a mistake. Even, if you use an invalid CSS declaration or an unsupported feature your browser will simply ignore the error and proceed to the next declaration. This can often be beneficial since a single error won't bring down your entire page -- the browser just won't display your content as expected. However, it can sometimes be difficult to figure out how to fix an improperly displayed element if you aren't sure what is causing the discrepancy. Fortunately, there are a couple of different ways to handle this issue.

The first way to try and debug a problematic web page is by using your browser's page inspector tool and CSS editor. To open up the page inspector tool, simply right click within a web page. In this example, we'll be using a Chrome browser to inspect one of the web pages you created in the previous chapter. If you aren't using Chrome, that's okay! Other browsers will offer you the same features, although they might be accessed in a slightly different way. With Chrome, once you right click within a web page, you simply need to choose "Inspect" from the pop up menu to open the page inspector tool. It will look something like this:

43

You can also use Ctrl + Shift + I to open the inspect panel in Google Chrome.

Now, take a look at the panel that has opened up. In the top portion, you can view the HTML that is used to display the page. In the lower right portion, you can view a graphical representation of each element's size, padding, border, and margin. In the lower left portion, you can see a block with tabs labeled Styles, Event Listeners, DOM Breakpoints, and Properties. We'll be working in the tab labeled Styles for this example.

To use the CSS Editor tool, first, click on an element in the top portion of the Inspect panel (where the HTML is displayed). For instance, let's click on the line that says <div class="news">. When you do so, you should see the contents of the Style tab below change to reflect the CSS that is used when displaying that element. If a CSS declaration is invalid for any reason, it will appear with a line through it in this window, along with a warning symbol. Also, if you hover over the attributes in this window, you will notice that they each have a checkbox to their left. You can click this checkbox to toggle the CSS attribute in the page.

Try this out now. Click the checkbox next to the text-align attribute and notice how this affects the way the news alert box displays on your web page on the left of the screen. The property will have a line

44

through it when you click the checkbox to toggle it off. If you click on the value to the right of the properties in the Style tab, you are given the option to enter a new value. You can also click on the colored boxes next to properties with a color value to change the color and instantly view how your page will be affected.

You can probably already understand how this can be a useful tool when trying to find and fix errors in your CSS. Not only can you instantly view any invalid CSS, you can easily manipulate the values for each of the properties of any element. By this, you can see how they affect how that element is displayed. You can easily view all of the CSS that is associated with an element.This is especially beneficial when working with elements that use multiple classes. You can even choose to temporarily ignore a certain property to check whether or not that is causing your page to display incorrectly. With these tools, you have a huge advantage in finding errors within your CSS over simply reading through your .css file manually!

If you'd rather not use the Page Inspector and CSS Editor in your browser, another option for finding errors in your CSS is to use a CSS Validator. You can find a CSS Validator online with a simple Google search. The validator should allow you to upload your CSS file, link to a web page online, or manually type some CSS into a text area. Then, the validator will comb through your CSS and display any errors it encounters along with the line numbers where they are located and the selectors that are associated with them. For instance, your CSS validator tool might tell you that there is an error in your .news class on line 35 that has occurred due to a missing semicolon or a misspelled property name.

Although using a CSS validator tool can be beneficial in some circumstances, there are many times it won't be able to provide you with the information you need to fix your display issues. For instance, if your page is displaying incorrectly because you typed the wrong value into your CSS file, the validator won't display an error since the syntax of the declaration is technically correct. Similarly, if you use the wrong selector when defining the styles for your page, the validator won't catch the error since nothing is syntactically incorrect. The best use of a CSS validator is probably as a precursor to using the Page Inspector method above -- the CSS validator will catch any basic errors in the syntax of your CSS, and you'll be able to fix them before addressing selector, property, and value issues with the built in browser CSS editor.

Try running a few of the examples from this book through a CSS validator and then view them with your browser's Inspect feature to familiarize yourself with both methods. That's it! Now you're ready to create, view, and debug your own HTML and CSS projects.

Chapter 5

CSS Animations

One of the cool and more recent things to come into CSS is the concept of CSS animations. CSS animations are great because they allow your site to be fluid and allow you to, as it sounds, animate your HTML code.

In the past, animating your code was pretty tedious. It was something you had to do through a combination of JavaScript code and clever CSS/HTML scripting. That or, in even older days, you'd have to animate your site through the use of Flash. This led to sites being extremely clunky, hard to interact with, tacky, and altogether much lower quality than they are today.

That all changed with the advent of CSS3. CSS3 now allows you to subtly animate your site in various ways that weren't available to programmers before. This is great because it means that there's an even greater chance that your site can be run without cumbersome scripts or anything of that nature.

The first part of CSS animations rests in keyframes. Keyframes allow you to set important events that happen throughout the course of an animation. You can name your keyframes and then refer to those at a later point. Let's say, for example, that we wanted to shift the text color from black to aqua. We could do this like so:

```
@keyframes myText {
    from {color: black;}
    to {color:yellow;}
}
```

You could then refer to this at a later point using *myText* as the animation name. You can give a certain animation description to an element by defining the animation name and then defining the length of the duration.

Note also that you can actually instead of using *from* and *to*, define the *percentages* at which these keyframes will take place. 0% describes the starting state, 100% describes the ending state, and anything between will ensure that the element takes on that property at that point within the overall duration of the animation.

Let's say we had an element called *myDiv* that we wanted to use our previous animation with:

```
#myDiv {
    animation-name: myText;
    animation-duration: 2s;
}
```

You can take this a step further by using CSS selectors. CSS selectors allow you to change the state of a given element when a certain event happens. Let's say, for example, that you wanted to specify an animation to happen exclusively when you hovered over a certain div. You could do so using the *hover* selector. Then, within the element description for the hover selector, you would put the animation data.

```
#myDiv {
    // raw data goes here
}
#myDiv:hover {
    animation-name: myText;
    animation-duration:2s;
}
```

This would cause the on-load data from the initial definition to happen when the page is loaded. The style of the element would change whenever the element was hovered over, thanks to the hover selector.

Therefore, whenever the element with the ID "myDiv" was hovered over, the specified animation would take place. Make sense? It's pretty simple!

There are a number of different CSS selectors that you can use.

hover will become active whenever the element is hovered over.

active is used in reference to anchor links and refers to the page that you're actively on. *a:active* will select any links on the page that link back to the page you are currently on and then style them in the way that you specify.

::after will insert data after the content of any given specified element.

::before will insert data before the content of any given specified element.

There are many more, but these are the most common ones and are therefore the ones that you are most likely going to be seeing often. Hover especially is the one that you'll most likely make the most use of.

With that, we've covered the basics of CSS animations. In the following chapter, we're going to be talking about how you can actually implement everything we've covered so far in this book in a few more modern web design paradigms. Stay tuned!

Chapter 6

Trends in CSS - Fixed Width Sites

One of the older trends in website design is actually essential to cover because it will give you a prime basis and starting point for the rest of your website design. One thing that we haven't really talked about at this point is actually culminating everything that you've worked with into a cohesive design, so we're going to be doing that in this chapter as we try to shamble together a lot of the concepts that we've covered into one bigger vision.

Web design is all about presentation. It's important that in your design path, you choose a way which presents your end vision in a way that makes it appealing to anybody who might come across your site. The most immediate way to get practice with this - and, indeed, the easiest - is to start with the most simple form of higher-level website design in CSS that is still applicable in today's web design market.

While you aren't going to come across many sites from established designers that utilize fixed-width constructions these days, it's still important that you understand the methodology and the thought process because it will actually teach you quite a bit about design in the process.

Fixed width designs have their basis in the fact that when you design a website, you want its presentation to be uniform. You want what the users see to be what you see. This can be difficult when you're dealing with all of the different computers and display resolutions out there. The way that early web designers would deal with this problem was by designing sites in such a way that anybody with any computer would see the same exact thing, provided that their viewport was beyond a certain width.

As at the time of writing this book, there really aren't many computers out there running on hardware updated enough to use a modern web browser that will have a smaller resolution than 1280x1024 - even mobile devices normally have a greater width than 960. If you go really old, such as iPhone second generation and prior, you'll run into widths that are in the 400s, but there's running on 10-year-old technology and very, very old mobile phones. So, you can trust that most people who would be accessing your site in the current climate would have a width greater than 960.

Most resolutions for computers generally have a width of at least 1366, with most desktop computers having a resolution width of at least 1920.

So what does this mean? This means that by finding a resolution that all of these devices can display and then show everything within that width, you assure that any device that has a resolution of that size or greater can display the content of your website in a seamless and uniform manner.

You've almost certainly in your time on the internet come across sites that do this in a pretty subtle way. One of the more popular web design magazines/periodicals, for example, uses this format in such a way that a given user would find it difficult to tell that this was the design principle. Because of the subtlety, regularity, and simplicity, this is a great place for future would-be web designers to start off.

So how does this work? The main philosophy of fixed-width design is having everything on your site fit within a certain container. This container sits on top of your background but contains all of your content. It will normally have a certain width affixed to it. A width of 900 or 1000 pixels is considered both standard and safe. Your code may end up looking like this:

```
<!DOCTYPE html>
<html>
    <head>
            <title>My site</title>
            <style>
                    html, body, background {
                            margin:0px;
                            padding:0px;
                            background:#d0d0d0;
                    }
                    #container {
                            width:900px;
                            margin-left:auto;
                            margin-right:auto;
                            border-left:1px solid #efefef;
                            border-right:1px solid #efefef;
                    }
            </style>
    </head>
    <body>
            <div id="container">
                    Container example.
            </div>
    </body>
</html>
```

The automatic left and right margins would center the div element. Your content would then fit pretty safely within this container. Your content could go in here and you could scale your content according to these widths. This means you could use exact pixel numbers and ensure that the design would actually look the same regardless of the platform that it was being viewed on. This is of the utmost importance in terms of overall usability and presentation and was, in fact, one of the main draws in using a fixed width design.

There are numerous drawbacks to using a fixed width design, though. The first of them is that it simply doesn't look as good as certain other kinds of designs do. For example, using exact widths means necessarily that your design won't be able to scale up to the beautiful and breathtaking artistic designs of the responsive designs that we'll be discussing in the next chapter.

This can be a massive drawback because as a web designer, you want your end result to look pretty. You want it to be flashy, effective, and showcase your abilities as well as the key point that the site is trying to convey. You want to show what you're able to do because web design is an artistic medium like any other form of design.

However, there are many cases where the simpler design and faster turnaround time and more exact and simplistic nature can be preferable. For example, many industrial designs will prefer, to one extent or another, the fixed-width design because it's less distracting and flashy. It lets people just do what they need to do with minimal intervention on the design side. It is an effective and simple design which gets out of the way and works even on older browsers and legacy systems.

Chapter 7

Trends In CSS - Responsive Design

The point of this book is to get you up to speed with CSS and feeling like you understand what you're doing. The hope is that by the end, you'll feel confident enough with the essential information pertaining to CSS and related disciplines that you'll be able to start designing your own sites.

One of the key parts of this is that we cover what could be considered the primary trends in CSS and web design at the moment. These are the most common as at the time of writing this book, but it does exclude certain frameworks which one could consider to be beyond the scope of this book, like React.JS or things similar in nature.

The first thing that we're going to talk about is *responsive web design*. Responsive web design arose in reaction to the trend of smartphone market dominance in web design. More and more people are having access to smartphones. They also have access to instantaneous web access regardless of where they were. Consequently, it began to become necessary to create intricate mobile designs which went beyond the low-data mobile versions of yesteryear from the eras of Blackberries and Palm Pres. In the face of high resolution mobile browsers and smartphones such as the iPhone and Samsung Galaxy, it was necessary to have a way for web design. This way, it could mimic the strengths of these mobile browsers and remove the need for a separate mobile version of the site. In the alternative, we are opting for a version of the site relative to the screen resolution of the device being used.

While this hasn't completely invalidated the mobile versions of sites, it does create a sort of situation where one can address them in a different way. Before, mobile sites were addressed by a JavaScript or HTML preprocessor directive that would cause the page to redirect if a certain browser was detected. With the advent of CSS3, it became possible to detect screen resolutions and automatically adjust the site in response rather than having a site being entirely readjusted.

Part of responsive design involves having designs that are artistically and aesthetically pleasing rather than just being fully functional. In this capacity, responsive designs serve as a means to make designs more expressive on the designer's end and more interactive and intuitive on the user's end.

So, what is responsive design? You've more than likely see the the responsive design before. If you've run into a web page that takes up the entire width and height of your browser window and that scales appropriately regardless of how large your browser window is at any given moment.

The way that responsive design works can take many different forms but the essence of responsive design comes down to essentially just everything being efficiently and easily scalable. It also should respond to the size of the viewport, or the overall viewing resolution of the browser. You can test out different viewport sizes in a responsive design by actually sizing your browser up and down both vertically and horizontally using your operating system's built-in sizing mechanisms.

Responsive designs work on the basis of things scaling with width and height values. You can accomplish this by using percentage-based sizing in your document. This is the basic idea, anyhow; the rest of it - which is a little bit beyond the scope of a beginner book - is actually using CSS commands in order to change the style of the document if, for example, the viewport were less than a certain width or height. For right now, we're just going to focus on how to implement scaling heights and widths.

The first thing you need to bear in mind is that when you test this out by scaling your window size up and down, you will notice that the size of the divisions will actually grow larger and smaller. This is perfect! It is exactly what is meant to happen.

The first thing that you need to realize about CSS width and height properties is that they inherit from the element larger than them. So, for example, you can't just say that divs of a certain class will have a height of, say, 20%. There is no definition of what 20% is even *of*. 20% of... what, exactly? In order for this statement to have any sort of meaning behind it, you need to realize that 20% is supposed to be a percentage of something else. If you say 20%, then this statement is somewhat inherently meaningless unless you indicate the 20% is a percentage of.

The way that you do this is by defining some parent object with a percentage. The greatest parent object is the *body* element, so any elements located within the *body* element can only be based on the *percentage* that is defined for the *body* element. Make sense? So if you want something to be 20%, then the body element has to have a parent height that this can be based on.

The body element will automatically use percentage based heights as a function of the viewport's size. However, if you were to define the body height as something like 1000 pixels, and had a div that was 20% height, then the div would base its 20% of the nearest parent element - here, body - and therefore have a height of 200 pixels.

Let's look at this a little bit more in-depth. The first thing you would have to do for scaling heights and widths is defined your body height as the height of the viewport. This will let everything else be a function of that when you define their heights and widths with percentages. In order to define your body as the height and width of the viewport, you're going to want to put the following in your code:

```
html, body, background {
    height:100%;
    width:100%;
}
```

Every div that you define afterward that has the body element as its most immediate parent element (as in, it isn't nested within another div element) will scale based on this. So, if you were to make a div now that was set to have a height of, say, 50%, it would take up 50% of the screen height.

In modern web design, this really comes to present itself in two different ways. The first is through the development of one-page designs, and the other way is through the development of grid-based design layouts. We'll spend a brief moment going over both of these so you have an idea of how they work.

One-page designs essentially are divided into sections. They'll usually have a splash opener to the site that talks about the site and its primary purpose, as well as a navigational bar or button you can click in order to open a navigational panel. Both of these will move with the page as you scroll down.

Now, you can start to move down the web page. Generally, all of the sections are the size of one viewport. There are often some neat transitions added in or other things that will cause the scrolling between sections to feel easy or even seamless. Others, still, will use parallax scrolling techniques in order to make the background stay exactly where it is as the user scrolls down the page.

Let's talk for a second about parallax scrolling before we move on to the next section of this chapter. Parallax scrolling is relatively intuitive and also pretty beautiful in its own right when done correctly. It's a snazzy feature that can be seriously cool when implemented well.

Parallax scrolling is essentially when the background moves in some way in response to the user scrolling. This runs counter to the standard wherein the background image or background of a given section doesn't necessarily stay with the user as they scroll. This might sound difficult, but it's actually rather simple.

You can implement parallax scrolling by setting a background image for the given section and then fix its position:

background-position: fixed;

This will lead the background position to scroll with the user as they move up and down the page. Interspersed with clever design, this can be an absolutely killer way to showcase your design abilities while not roughing up your code or making it excessively difficult. Bare this in mind, because this is a massive trend in web design these days and you're going to be seeing it a lot.

Through other CSS features and JavaScript events, you can add even more things to implement within your code base which will make your design more appealing or more intuitive. The combination of HTML5, CSS3, and JavaScript is extremely powerful. Some people have even created full-on games in just these 3 languages. So, it's important that you have a grasp on them and how they work because by doing so, you're setting yourself up for success in terms of long-term design potential.

The other way that these responsive designs tend to be implemented is through the use of grid-based layouts. Grid-based layouts are becoming more and more common as time presses on. Their particular handiness comes from the fact that, first and foremost, they offer a very convenient modular method of development. Moreover, they allow you to design a simple and beautiful site using pre-developed and prefixed dimensions. This makes your entire development process far easier.

An example of a grid-based layout would be something which, for example, uses a 3 wide grid where 3 elements are fit into one row. In addition, these rows are roughly 30% width each, perhaps with a 3% margin on either side and a 2% margin in between. This would allow the information to be presented in a clean and pragmatic manner.

The grid-based layout is one of the other very popular methods of design because it allows for the combination of multiple different manners of layouts within the context of a grid-based system.

Grid-based designs fill, to some degree, the industrial void that fixed-width sites used to fill. While fixed-width sites do still exist, when simple and effective designs that look modern are needed, they are usually accomplished using some form of grid-based design. This also is an ideal choice for online store fronts because it's unpretentious and rather easy to use.

With that, we've covered the other monolith of modern web design: the responsive website. As I said, there's quite a bit more to it than all of this, but it's something that you're mainly going to get experience and exposure to through practice.

Conclusion

Thank you again for purchasing *CSS: Basic Fundamental Guide For Beginners*, and congratulations on making it to the end! Hopefully, you've gained some insight into how to use CSS selectors, discovered how to effectively create layouts for your web pages, and had some fun exploring the different ways CSS can enhance your websites.

The next step is to let yourself be creative. Have an idea for a unique new web page? Try to apply the techniques you learned throughout this book to make it a reality! Practice makes perfect, just like with any other skill, so be sure to put in the time to polish your techniques. There are countless new websites out there just waiting for someone to create them, and that means countless opportunities for you to hone your skills.

Finally, if you found this book useful as you began on your CSS journey, please take a moment to review it on Amazon. Thank you, good luck, and enjoy your new and improved websites!

www.ingramcontent.com/pod-product-compliance
Lightning Source LLC
Chambersburg PA
CBHW070857070326
40690CB00009B/1883